Praying the Rosary

This is ~~...~~ lovely
prayer book called
"Jesus Christ, The Way, The Truth,
The Life"
which I have been using the
last few weeks

The complete book contains
Morning and Night prayer and
other short meditations and
proved invaluable, these last
weeks for the occasions when
I can do it long on because
ordinary ... discipline (if there
such a thing!) is beyond me.
& think the Meditation on
the beatitudes is beautiful.

Christmas '86

Praying the Rosary

with

The Beatitudes

The Way of the Cross

and

An Examination of Conscience

DAVID KONSTANT

Collins

Collins Liturgical Publications
8 Grafton Street, London W1X 3LA

Distributed in Ireland by
Educational Company of Ireland
21 Talbot Street, Dublin 1

Collins Liturgical Australia
PO Box 3023, Sydney 2001

© 1981 David Konstant
First published as part of
Jesus Christ, The Way, The Truth, The Life

First published in this edition 1985
Third Printing 1986
ISBN 0 00 599849 2

Nihil obstat: Anton Cowan
Imprimatur: Philip Harvey, Bishop in North London Westminster,
5 January 1981

Made and printed in Great Britain
by Bell and Bain Ltd, Glasgow

Contents

Acknowledgements

The publishers are grateful for permission to use the following copyright material:

Quotations from the Bible are from *Jerusalem Bible,* © 1966, 1967 and 1968, Darton, Longman & Todd, and Doubleday & Co, Inc.

A Meditation on the Way of the Cross was originally published by Catholic Truth Society, London.

An Examination of Conscience is based on one originally published in *A Penitent's Prayer Book* by Mayhew McCrimmon Ltd.

The illustrations for the Stations of the Cross are by Philip le Bas, and stand in the church of Our Lady of the Visitation, Greenford, Middlesex.

Photos:
   Noeline Kelly, p 9
   G. Chapman, p 41
   Christopher Smedley, pp 61, 91

PREFACE

The spire at Salisbury Cathedral is one of the finest in the world. It is a surprise to learn that the original wooden scaffolding is still inside it. Although it is no longer needed it has somehow become a part of the spire. A prayer book like this is a little like the scaffolding. The meditations are a skeleton around which you build your own prayers. To begin with they are someone else's prayers, but as you repeat them they become truly your own and may provide a beginning for your own conversations with God, your own building.

The Rosary helps us meditate on some of the great events of our Lord's life, death and glory. Mary, who was part of these events, can be the vehicle for our own reflections.

In the Joyful Mysteries she catches for us the intimacy of the incarnation through the Annunciation, Visitation, Birth and Presentation of Jesus. And she leaves us marvelling at that extraordinary mystery pointed to by the Finding in the Temple — the thirty unknown years. Like her we are invited to ponder all these things in our hearts.

In the Sorrowful Mysteries we journey with her on the stony road to Calvary. We are made aware of the tragedy of betrayal and of the agony that inevitably accompanies it. We feel with her the pain of compassion and wonder once again at the mystery of the death of the Son of God.

Meditating on the Glorious Mysteries we begin to understand that Resurrection is only possible where there has been death. The grain of wheat must die if it is to bear fruit. And so we walk with Mary to discover a lasting joy — the fruit that comes to all the saints of God.

The Beatitudes are at first sight so contradictory that we may be tempted to ignore them. How can someone who is mourning be happy? Why should the poor be blessed? Surely no one can be perfect? Then we begin to see through the apparent contradictions and to discover why the Beatitudes are the basis for the Christian's daily living. The more they form part of our prayer the more we may find how closely they refer to our lives.

One part of life we can never escape is its hardships. Whoever we are, sooner or later we experience pain, sorrow, and frustrations. We all have a cross to carry. Meditating on our Lord's *Way of the Cross* can help us discover that even in our agonies we may perhaps find peace and contentment of soul.

And finally in this book there is an invitation to us to look at ourselves honestly, to make an *examination of conscience.* This is especially to help us go to confession and celebrate our forgiveness by God in the Sacrament of Penance.

I hope that this small scaffolding for prayer will help you in your building. A cathedral spire however beautiful cannot reach heaven. But the building you make by your prayer is one where God truly dwells.

David Konstant
December, 1984

A Meditation on the Mysteries of the Rosary

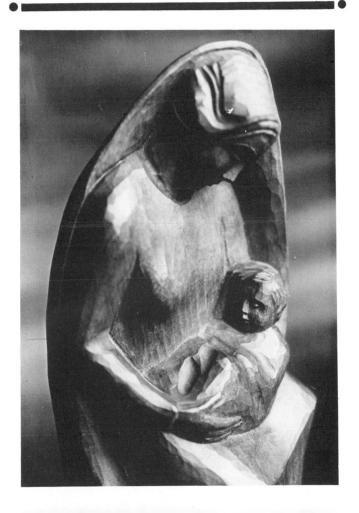

The Joyful Mysteries

THE ANNUNCIATION

The angel Gabriel was sent by God to a town in Galilee
called Nazareth, to a virgin betrothed to a man named
Joseph, and the virgin's name was Mary. He went in and
said to her, 'Rejoice, so highly favoured! The Lord is with
you. You are to conceive and bear a son, and you must
name him Jesus. He will be great and will be called Son
of the Most High.' Mary said to the angel, 'But how can
this come about, since I am a virgin?' 'The Holy Spirit
will come upon you' the angel answered, 'and the power
of the Most High will cover you with its shadow. And so
the child will be holy and will be called Son of God.' 'I am
the handmaid of the Lord,' said Mary 'let what you have
said be done to me.' And the angel left her.

from Luke 1: 26–38

What a frightening invitation, to become mother of
    such a child . . .
  a child of infinite promise.
One can imagine the sudden clutch of fear . . .
  the puzzlement . . .
  the anxiety about the future.
Surely he doesn't really mean me?
  But in a moment the fears are stilled,
  and all is seen to be possible.
  'Be it done to me according to your word.'

What is my annunciation? When has God sent his
angel to me to announce his Good News? And how have
I reacted to the promises he has made to me?

God's messengers do come to me;
    they tell me that I'm highly favoured . . .
    much graced and blessed . . .
    with much fruit to bear . . .
    and they tell me too that the Lord is with me.

But often I do not recognise God's friends,
    because their words are so demanding,
    and I am afraid.

Everyone is blessed by God . . .
    he has no favourites.
God is with all his people . . .
    he cannot forget any one of them.
All are chosen people . . .
    each one unique . . .
    every person special.
'Do not be afraid,' he says to me 'for I have redeemed
you; I have called you by your name and you are mine.'

I have been called by God to do him some definite
      service . . .
I have a vocation to become what he calls me to be.
If I am ever to answer this call
    I must learn to say,
    'Yes . . . Let it be done . . . Let it be done . . .
    Let it be done to me according to your word.'

I must let go –
    of fear . . .
    of a sense of inadequacy . . .
    of selfishness and pride . . .
    of wanting to have everything planned before I make
      a move.
Then I may learn to trust in God; who is Father,
Friend, Tremendous Lover; who knows what I can do;
and to whom nothing is impossible.

Speak, Lord, your servant hears!

———————

THE VISITATION

Mary set out and went as quickly as she could to a town in the hill country of Judah. She went to Zechariah's house and greeted Elizabeth. Now as soon as Elizabeth heard Mary's greeting, the child leapt in her womb and Elizabeth was filled with the Holy Spirit. She gave a loud cry and said, 'Of all women you are the most blessed, and blessed is the fruit of your womb. Why should I be honoured with a visit from the mother of my Lord? For the moment your greeting reached my ears, the child in my womb leapt for joy. Yes, blessed is she who believed that the promise made her by the Lord would be fulfilled.' Mary stayed with Elizabeth about three months and then went back home. Luke 1: 39–45, 56

It is a sign of generosity to be willing to share in another's happiness. Mary's first thought after the angel had left her was to visit her cousin Elizabeth, who 'in her old age had herself conceived a son'.

There was respect in this visit . . .
    also thoughtfulness . . .
    and a certain delicacy.

Elizabeth was an older woman . . . perhaps she was un-sure of the future . . . she must have welcomed the help and companionship . . . all Mary could give were her time and herself . . . gifts that really count.

The generous gift brings a heartfelt response:
    'Blessed is she who believed
    that the promise made her by the Lord
    would be fulfilled.'

This is another Beatitude:
I am really blessed if I believe
    in the love of God, which enfolds me . . .

in the truth of his Word, which speaks to me . . .
in the power of his Spirit, which overshadows me.
Then I shall know that the 'Almighty has done great
things for me', and that I shall live for ever.

First, though, I have to believe in others . . .
and this means that I must visit them and meet them –
not just casually in the hairdresser's, or the pub, or the
    office or factory, or on the doorstep,
where all we talk about is football, the weather, cars or
    the way prices are rising . . .
but generously, so as to take them into my heart . . .
and share with them something of myself.

This is hard to do . . .
I have been taught to protect myself with
    my privacy . . .
    my shyness . . .
    my self-imposed loneliness . . .
    my property.

If only I can take the risk
    to be open to others . . .
    to be patient with them . . .
    to waste time with them . . .
    to listen to them,
then I shall learn to believe in them, and they to
    believe in me.

This takes time . . . more even than three months . . .
and love . . . but the reward is God himself . . . for God
is love.

Teach me, Lord, to give myself generously for others.

———————

THE BIRTH OF OUR LORD

Joseph travelled up to Bethlehem to be registered together with Mary, his betrothed, who was with child. While they were there the time came for her to have her child, and she gave birth to a son, her first-born. She wrapped him in swaddling clothes, and laid him in a manger because there was no room for them at the inn. The angel of the Lord appeared to some shepherds close by, and said, 'Today in the town of David a saviour has been born to you; he is Christ the Lord.' The shepherds said to one another, 'Let us go to Bethlehem and see this thing that has happened which the Lord has made known to us.' So they hurried away and found Mary and Joseph, and the baby lying in the manger, and they went back glorifying and praising God for all they had heard and seen.

> The Word was made flesh,
> he lived among us.

from Luke 2: 1–20; John 1: 14

Every birth is truly a miracle. Each birth marks God's entry into the world. A new-born child is made in the image of God, he is made for God, and he is only fully alive when he knows God as his Father in heaven.

This birth is the perfect sign that God is with us.
God has spoken.
His Word has been given to the world.

This is a mystery to ponder . . .
    a wonder to marvel at . . .
    a glory to sing about.
'Glory to God in the highest, and peace to his people on
    earth.'

It scarcely seems credible that this child,
    born in such simplicity . . .
    recognised by only a handful of shepherds . . .
should be Saviour . . . Son of God . . . God-with-us . . .

the Image of the invisible God . . .
the last revelation of God to man.

But so he is.

I need to understand that God reveals himself to the
    poor and simple . . .
that it is the ordinary things of life –
    a smile, a word;
    forgiveness, freedom;
    life itself and the whole of creation –
which show the grandeur of God . . .
that it is because he was born in poverty and simplicity
that I have the courage to approach him, for he is like
me in all things except sin.

Many of my friends are searching for God, but perhaps
I do not show them where to look for him, or how to
recognise him. Unwittingly I may have become a
barrier to their faith,
    by my unwillingness to talk about God . . .
    by my ignorance of the Gospel message . . .
    by my empty materialism.

What my friends are looking for is often so simple . . .
        so ordinary . . . and so human,
    that I have not grasped that their search is truly
    for God, the Word made flesh.

Let me try to become a better witness to God's
        presence,
    to see him in the world he has made . . .
    to meet him in my fellow men . . .
    to know him through his eternal Word . . .
and so to proclaim him by my daily living.

May Christ be born in me today.

THE PRESENTATION

Mary and Joseph took Jesus up to Jerusalem to present him to the Lord. When they brought in the child Jesus to do for him what the Law required, Simeon took him into his arms and blessed God; and he said:
'Now my eyes have seen the salvation
which you have prepared for all the nations to see,
a light to enlighten the pagans
and the glory of your people Israel.'
He said to Mary, 'This child is destined to be a sign that is rejected – and a sword will pierce your own soul too.'
The Word was the true light
that enlightens all men.
He came to his own domain
and his own people did not accept him.

from Luke 2: 22–35; John 1: 9, 11

All belongs to God. He is the Creator. Everything comes from him and in due course returns to him. 'Every good and perfect gift comes from above, from the Father of all light.' Mary and Joseph knew that their wonderful gift was from God . . . and must be brought back to him. Simeon saw that the child would dispel the world's darkness . . . though through suffering and rejection.

What child is this?
His parents could not see into the future . . .
    could not know the life he would lead . . .
    or the death he would suffer . . .
    could not imagine the richness of the one in their
        care.
They knew he was called by God,
and so they did for him what God's Law required.

Of any infant we may ask, 'What child is this?'.
We can never fathom the mystery of another . . .
    or know his future . . .
    or map his journey.

All we know for certain is that he is called by God and that we who have care for him must do as God's Law requires.

We may learn from God:
'When you were a child I loved you.
I myself taught you to walk,
I took you in my arms;
I led you with reins of kindness,
with leading-strings of love.'
This is the Law . . . to love.

What is God's plan for me?
'In God's plan *person*
every single man is called upon to grow.
Each life is a vocation.
From birth, each one of us carries within himself
the seeds of personal growth.
Each one of us can bear the fruit
proposed for him by God.' *Is he with God.*
All have common vocation -
Like Christ, I am called to enlighten the world, and so must be ready,
to be rejected . . .
to be misunderstood . . .
to suffer hardship for justice's sake . . .
to be without honour among my own people.

I must first be pruned . . . bear much fruit . . . and so return to God enriched.

O Lord be praised for what I am, and what I may become!

_____

THE FINDING IN THE TEMPLE

Every year his parents used to go to Jerusalem for the feast of the Passover. When he was twelve years old, they went up for the feast as usual. When they were on their way home after the feast, the boy Jesus stayed behind in Jerusalem without his parents knowing it. Three days later, they found him in the Temple, sitting among the doctors, listening to them, and asking them questions; and all those who heard him were astounded at his intelligence and his replies. They were overcome when they saw him, and his mother said to him, 'My child, why have you done this to us? See how worried your father and I have been, looking for you.' 'Why were you looking for me?' he replied 'Did you not know that I must be busy with my Father's affairs?' But they did not understand what he meant. He then went down with them and came to Nazareth and lived under their authority. His mother stored up all these things in her heart. And Jesus increased in wisdom, in stature, and in favour with God and men.   Luke 2: 41–43, 46–52

At first sight the incident is inexplicable. It is uncharacteristic . . . it seems to show thoughtlessness and even selfishness. But perhaps it can help me to realise how necessary it is

to let another grow . . .
to encourage him to be independent . . .
to give him room to be free . . .
to offer care without constraint . . .
to understand commitment to what is important . . .
to be ready always to listen to the questions being asked.

Jesus was a boy. Like all young people he needed to know himself . . . to find himself . . . and to become in his humanity what his Father was calling him to be. 'Did you not know that I must be busy with my Father's affairs? . . . My meat is to do the will of my Father in heaven.'

18

He listened and questioned.
There is a model for me.

What are the right questions for me to ask? Even to
know the questions, I must first listen to God
    in prayer . . .
    in the words of scripture . . .
    in the Church's teaching . . .
    in the advice of God's friends . . .
    in the wonder of his creation . . .
    in the voice of conscience.
As I listen, so I shall learn to question well.

Jesus grew 'in wisdom, in stature, and in favour with
    God and men'.
This is my ambition, too – to grow.
Let me realise that
while God gives the increase,
I myself have a part to play
so that growth may be possible.

I need
    to be open to the Holy Spirit, so I may repent and be
      converted . . .
    to take proper care of myself, so I may have the
      energy to do God's work . . .
    to be willing to know others, so I may meet the risen,
      living Christ . . .
    to take time to ponder God's word, so I may learn
      true wisdom.

Then I will come to know myself . . . to find myself . . .
and to become what the Father is calling me to be.

      Lord, give me the patience to grow.

The Sorrowful Mysteries

THE AGONY IN THE GARDEN

When the Passover meal was over, Jesus left to make his way as usual to the Mount of Olives, to a small estate called Gethsemane, with the disciples following. Then he withdrew from them, about a stone's throw away, and knelt down and prayed. 'Father', he said, 'if you are willing take this cup away from me. Nevertheless, let your will be done, not mine.' Then an angel appeared to him, coming from heaven to give him strength. In his anguish he prayed even more earnestly, and his sweat fell to the ground like great drops of blood. When he rose from prayer he went to the disciples and found them sleeping for sheer grief. 'Why are you asleep?' he said to them. 'Get up and pray not to be put to the test.'

Luke 22: 39–46

Why didn't Jesus escape from his enemies? Was there any need for him to go through all this? Could he not have left quietly until the commotion had died down? This is the temptation that comes to us all at one time or another.

to avoid the issue . . .

to choose the easy way out . . .

to run away from what is right . . .

But there are some problems that simply have to be faced.

The cup has to be drained . . . the burden must be carried . . .

the needs of others must take first place.

Jesus, like us, prayed that he could be spared . . . he was in an agony of apprehension and fear so that he sweated blood. His prayer was answered: 'Not my will, but yours be done'.

In my agony, let this become my prayer.

In the agony
   of frustration, when it seems there is nothing I can do to ease the situation . . .
   of being misunderstood, when it's as if the whole world has turned its back on me . . .
   of shame, when my sins and failures overshadow the whole of life . . .
   of anxiety, when my responsibilities seem too great for me to bear . . .
   of apprehension, when the oncoming horror is too dreadful for me to face . . .
   of sadness, when someone I love turns against me and friendship dies . . .

Indeed I may pray not to be put to the test, and to be spared from such pain. But there are times when
   as a result of sin . . .
   or error . . .
   or accident . . .
   or sickness . . .
   or because of human weakness and limitation . . .
   or because of what my neighbour needs,
I shall undergo a fearful agony.

Then may I pray that I can know and accept God's will.

Lord, the spirit is willing, but the flesh is weak!

THE SCOURGING AT THE PILLAR

Pilate said to the chief priests and the elders, 'What am I to do with Jesus who is called Christ?' They all said, 'Let him be crucified!' 'Why?' he asked 'What harm has he done? He has done nothing that deserves death, so I shall have him flogged and let him go.' But they shouted all the louder, 'Let him be crucified!' Then Pilate saw that he was making no impression, that in fact a riot was imminent. So he took some water, washed his hands in front of the crowd and said, 'I am innocent of this man's blood. It is your concern.' He ordered Jesus to be first scourged and then handed over to be crucified.

from Matthew 27: 21–26; Luke 23: 15

When people are frightened there is no depth to which they won't sink. The chief priests were frightened because

Jesus was prepared to take the law into his own hands: 'the sabbath was made for man, not man for the sabbath' . . .

Jesus was popular with the ordinary people: 'his teaching made a deep impression on them because, unlike the scribes, he taught them with authority' . . .

Pilate was frightened because

Jesus was an enigma, whose kingdom was 'not of this world' . . .

Jesus bore witness to the truth, and the truth is uncomfortable for those whose lives are a lie . . .

So the Jews demanded his death, and Pilate looked for a compromise.

'He has done nothing that deserves death, so I shall have him flogged' . . . a sop to the Establishment . . . a ruthless injustice . . . 'it is expedient that one man should die for the people'.

How often are we prepared to allow an injustice because,

it is too much trouble to do anything about it . . .

we don't have the power to effect a worthwhile change . . .

we accept the law as our first obligation . . .

we are afraid to accept the truth . . .

material affairs outweigh the spiritual.

We pass by on the other side of the road, and avert our eyes.

Let me remember the pain endured by so many of my fellow men,

the distress of the sick; who look for my presence . . .

the suffering of the handicapped; who wait for my visits . . .

the timidity of the lonely; who hope for my friendship . . .

the anguish of the starving; who trust for my bread . . .

the heartache of the homeless; whose future looks so empty . . .

the emptiness of the sad; whose happiness is in my hands . . .

the despair of the falsely imprisoned; who plead for my help . . .

'Behold, the man!'

Jesus, the suffering one,
is present in all those who suffer,
and I, if I have faith, have the power to heal them.

Lord, give me the strength to bind up broken hearts.

———————

THE CROWNING WITH THORNS

The governor's soldiers took Jesus with them. Then they stripped him and made him wear a scarlet cloak, and having twisted some thorns into a crown they put this on his head and placed a reed in his right hand. To make fun of him they knelt to him saying, 'Hail, king of the Jews!' And they spat on him and took the reed and struck him on the head with it.   Matthew 27: 27–30

Mockery is often more hurtful than the hurt that attends it.

> When Jesus Christ was yet a child
> He had a garden small and wild,
> Wherein he cherished roses fair,
> And wove them into garlands there.
>
> Now once, as summer-time drew nigh,
> There came a troop of children by,
> And seeing roses on the tree,
> With shouts they plucked them merrily.
>
> 'Do you bind roses in your hair?'
> They cried, in scorn, to Jesus there.
> The boy said humbly: 'Take, I pray,
> All but the naked thorns away.'
>
> Then of the thorns they made a crown,
> And with rough fingers pressed it down,
> Till on his forehead fair and young
> Red drops of blood like roses sprung.
>
> Plechtcheev

I know it's not a perfect world and that envy, jealousy and hatred can be found everywhere:
    'a sour suspicion born of fear that the other man is finer . . .

a subtle rumour breeding news that another's love is
    sweeter . . .
a tangled knowledge canker-grown that the stran-
    ger's path is straighter . . .
a numb awareness vainly fought that the weaker
    man's my leader.'
These, maybe, are the thorns in my crown.

But I do have a crown of roses . . . as well as thorns. My
crown is woven of
    my friends, whose constancy and love urge me to
        generosity . . .
    my faith, a grace from God which tugs at me to know
        him . . .
    my forgiveness, a sign of God's love that confirms my
        hope . . .

Wearing such a crown I may learn
    to soften the thorns of selfishness . . .
    to be happy with the gifts I have received . . .
    to rejoice in the talents and success of others.

'Glory to God in the highest, and peace to his people
on earth.'

———————

THE CARRYING OF THE CROSS

Pilate handed Jesus over to the Jews to be crucified. They then took charge of him, and carrying his own cross he went out of the city to the place of the skull or, as it was called in Hebrew, Golgotha. As they were leading him away they seized on a man, Simon from Cyrene, who was coming in from the country, and made him shoulder the cross and carry it behind Jesus. Large numbers of people followed him, and of women, too, who mourned and lamented for him. But Jesus turned on them and said, 'Daughters of Jerusalem, do not weep for me; weep rather for yourselves and for your children.'

John 19: 17; Luke 23: 26–28

This was Jesus's last pilgrimage. His life had been marked by journeys:
  the flight to Egypt . . .
  the visit as a child to Jerusalem . . .
  and later his missionary journeys to all parts of
     Palestine to tell his fellow countrymen about his
     Father.
Calvary was to be the final staging post.

He had told his followers,
  'Take up your cross daily and follow me' . . .
  'Come to me all you who labour and are over-
     burdened, and I will refresh you' . . .
  'My yoke is easy and my burden light'.

It is said that the condemned prisoner carried only the cross piece, which was lashed to his arms . . . the vertical post stayed in position at the top of the hill.

The horizontal – a reminder
  that like Christ I am on a pilgrim journey . . .
  that like Christ I cannot always choose the way . . .
  that like Christ I carry with me a burden I cannot
     lose . . .

The vertical – a reminder
   that God is always there . . .
   that all I do is in the end to give him glory . . .
   that my journey to heaven must be rooted in the
      ground . . .

If my life is really a pilgrimage to God, carrying the
weight of myself, it is sensible
   to abandon unnecessary trifles so as not to be en-
      cumbered
     for I cannot serve God and material things . . .
   to be willing to lay the axe to the root of the tree and
      be converted,
     for to be perfect is to have changed often . . .
   to accept the company of others, their consolation and
      their help,
     for on my own I am powerless . . .
The road is rough and the falls are many.

God draws me towards himself, for
   his love is patient . . .
   my baptism has marked me out for him . . .
   my heart knows no rest until it rests in him.

     Lord, see that I do not follow the wrong path
      and lead me in the path of life eternal.

—————————

THE CRUCIFIXION

When they reached the place called The Skull, they crucified him there and the two criminals also, one on the right, the other on the left. Jesus said, 'Father forgive them; they do not know what they are doing'. Then they cast lots to share out his clothing. When the sixth hour came there was darkness over the whole land until the ninth hour. And at the ninth hour Jesus cried out in a loud voice, 'My God, my God, why have you deserted me?' Then he said, 'Father, into your hands I commit my spirit'. With these words he breathed his last. When the centurion saw what had taken place, he gave praise to God and said, 'This was a great and good man'. And when all the people who had gathered for the spectacle saw what had happened, they went home beating their breasts. All his friends stood at a distance; so also did the women who had accompanied him from Galilee, and they saw all this happen.

Luke 23: 33–34, 46–49; Mark 15: 33–34

Death is inescapable, but this does not make it any the less frightening. Jesus himself was afraid, and even felt for a time that he had been forgotten by his Father. There can be no worse horror than believing ourselves to have been abandoned. Such an experience can come to anyone, when

God, and faith in God seem to have vanished . . .
friends stand at a distance, and don't want to know us . . .
all those we have relied on for support suddenly have nothing to offer . . .

At moments like this I must remind myself that dying should be a daily experience if the last enemy, death itself, is to be conquered.
Jesus said:

'Unless the wheat grain falls on the ground and dies
it remains only a single grain

but if it dies
it yields a rich harvest . . .
Anyone who finds his life will lose it;
anyone who loses his life for my sake will find it . . .'

If I am to learn the art of living, I must practise the art of dying. 'Death is swallowed up in victory' . . . it is a threshold to new life.

To die is to let go,
of prejudices, vanities and my own opinion . . .
of those ambitions that turn me from what is worth-while . . .
of the things, the comforts and even the people who distract me from God . . .

To die is to become obedient,
to God's commandments . . .
to the needs of others . . .
to the demands of the present moment . . .

To die is to empty myself . . . to belong to others . . . to cast aside the inessential . . . to leave something to God . . . to abandon myself: 'Father, into your hands I commit my spirit'.

At death there are no more tomorrows . . . but only a memory of yesterdays . . . and an eternal present.

Then I shall truly know that God has not forgotten me, and that I am safe in his hands.

Lord, teach me how to die.

———————————

The Glorious Mysteries

THE RESURRECTION

On the first day of the week, at the first sign of dawn, the women went to the tomb with the spices they had prepared. They found that the stone had been rolled away from the tomb, but on entering discovered that the body of the Lord Jesus was not there. As they stood there not knowing what to think, two men in brilliant clothes suddenly appeared at their side. Terrified, the women lowered their eyes. But the two men said to them, 'Why look among the dead for someone who is alive?' He is not here; he has risen. Remember what he told you when he was still in Galilee: that the Son of Man had to be handed over into the power of sinful men and be crucified, and rise again on the third day?' And they remembered his words.   Luke 24: 1–8

The apostles were, to our way of thinking, slow to believe the full message of the Gospel. 'Did you not know,' the risen Christ said to the despondent couple on the road to Emmaus 'that the Christ had to suffer and so enter into his glory?'

Wake up from your sleep
rise from the dead
and Christ will shine on you.

He died,
so that his Father might raise him to a new life . . .
so that all of us could be brought alive in Christ.
St Paul says, 'If Christ is not risen our faith is in vain'.

Let me notice the small reminders in my ordinary life that point the way to a richer life with God . . . and give thanks to him for

the simple pleasure of food and drink . . .

the security of shelter and home . . .

the tranquillity of sleep and quiet . . .

Let me appreciate the emergence of new life that is a daily miracle for all its frequency and inevitability . . . and praise God for

the coming to birth of a new day . . .

the beauty produced by the work of human hands . . .

the recovery of strength after sickness . . .

and above all, the birth of a child . . .

Let me marvel at the brief resurrections I experience in my struggle to follow Christ . . . and thank God for

forgiveness, after failure and sin . . .

praise, when all I had expected was to be un-
noticed . . .

trust, when I knew it was undeserved . . .

welcome, in spite of my selfish isolation.

All of this is an anticipation and promise of what is to come . . . which eye has not seen . . . nor ear heard . . . which has not entered into the heart of man.

If I want to be alive I must 'eat the flesh of the Son of Man and drink his blood' . . . I must do as he did . . . in memory of him. My communion with him at Mass is the perfect foretaste of what is to come and the source of the resurrection I must search for:

The Sacred Banquet

in which Christ is received . . .

the memory of his Passion recalled . . .

the mind filled with grace . . .

and a pledge of future glory given.

'Lord, that I may live, and live to the full!'

———————

THE ASCENSION

May the God of our Lord Jesus Christ, the Father of glory, give you a spirit of wisdom and perception of what is revealed, to bring you to full knowledge of him. May he enlighten the eyes of your mind so that you can see what hope his call holds for you, what rich glories he has promised the saints will inherit and how infinitely great is the power that he has exercised for us believers. This you can tell from the strength of his power at work in Christ, when he used it to raise him from the dead and to make him sit at his right hand, in heaven. He has put all things under his feet, and made for him, as the ruler of everything, the head of the Church; which is his body, the fullness of him who fills the whole creation.

Jesus said to the apostles, 'All authority in heaven and on earth has been given to me. Go, therefore, make disciples of all the nations; baptise them in the name of the Father and of the Son and of the Holy Spirit, and teach them to observe all the commands I gave you. And know that I am with you always; yes, to the end of time.'

Ephesians 1: 17–23; Matthew 28: 18–20

Jesus is now with his Father . . . continually interceding on our behalf. But he is alive too in all the members of his Body, the Church . . . he fills them with his own life . . . he encourages, forgives, guides . . . he helps the whole of creation to achieve its purpose.

The Master Craftsman has given his apprentices all he can . . . it is for them now, under his care, to continue his work . . . to witness . . . to heal . . . to set free those who are enslaved. Much has been entrusted to us.

I'm scared of such great responsibility,
    'You can't mean me to do this, Lord' . . .
    'Lord, I am not worthy' . . .
    'I do not know how to speak, Lord: I'm only a
        child' . . .

I want to hide and leave it to those who are better fitted: the bishops . . . the priests . . . the nuns . . . the clever ones . . . the holy ones. And all he says to me is

'Do not be afraid, for I have redeemed you . . .
I have called you by your name . . .
and you are mine.'

I am part of the body of Christ . . . there are all sorts of service to be done . . . but it is the same God who is working in all of them . . . I cannot say 'Christ has no need of me' . . . my place, my work, my mission are indispensable . . . I need not be fainthearted, because Jesus Christ is working in me . . . with him all things are possible.

I must be ready then to be a witness to the power of Christ in me,

by hearing his word and keeping it . . .
by making his teaching my own . . .
by spreading the Gospel by word and action . . .
by practising justice and integrity . . .
by readiness to take up my cross daily . . .
by faithfulness to my daily prayer . . .

If he is on my side . . . I have nothing to fear.

My witness may be silent . . . but it will be nonetheless strong and effective.

'O Lord, open my lips;
and my tongue shall announce your praise!'

———————————

THE COMING OF THE HOLY SPIRIT

I shall ask the Father, and he will give you another
Advocate to be with you for ever. The Advocate, the Holy
Spirit, whom the Father will send in my name, will teach
you everything and remind you of all I have said to you.
When the Spirit of truth comes he will lead you to the
complete truth.

When Pentecost day came round, they had all met in one
room, when suddenly they heard what sounded like a
powerful wind from heaven, the noise of which filled the
entire house in which they were sitting; and something
appeared to them that seemed like tongues of fire; these
separated and came to rest on the head of each of them.
They were all filled with the Holy Spirit, and began to
speak foreign languages as the Spirit gave them the gift
of speech.   John 14: 16, 26; 16: 23; Acts 2: 1–4

God's mystery is gradually unfolded. He is Father . . .
the Creator . . . the one who holds all things in being
. . . the Shepherd of his people . . . the Bridegroom.

He is Son . . . the Son of God made man . . . the Word
made flesh . . . the image of the invisible God . . . who
died so that we might live.

He is Holy Spirit . . . sent by the Father and the Son . . .
Advocate . . . Helper . . . Breath of Life . . . who comes
to everyone who invites him. The Spirit of God is man's
partner . . . he enobles . . . teaches . . . directs.

The gifts of the Spirit cannot be counted . . . they are as
many as there are people in the world, and more be-
sides . . . but among them we can number,
    the wisdom of the man who knows real worth when
        he finds it . . .
    the understanding of a mother who can reach her
        daughter's heart . . .

the judgement of the youngster who reads a situation with uncomplicated simplicity . . .

the courage of the one who is prepared to swim against the stream . . .

the knowledge of the man of prayer whose faith and peace are unshakeable . . .

the unfathomable respect of a son for his father, and of a father for his son . . .

The cheerfulness of the dying . . . the generosity of the poor . . . the angry fire of the prophet . . . the patience of the teacher . . . the smile of a friend . . . the sorrow of a sinner . . . the compassion of the one who forgives.

The disciples of Jesus were dispirited . . . they had lost heart . . . the bottom had dropped out of their lives . . . the urgency of the gospel had disappeared . . . they were filled with fear. 'What can we do?' . . . 'Is God still with us?' . . . 'What will happen to us?' . . .

Then the Spirit came and all was changed. They were enlivened . . . inspired . . . encouraged . . . renewed. They were eager with the fire of unselfish love . . . alive with the rhythm of a new beginning . . . confident in the discovery of truth.

I must look for my personal Pentecost . . . ready to accept the Spirit when he comes . . . willing to be converted . . . happy to abandon myself to his urgent leadership . . . so that there may grow in me the Christian instinct for truth . . . love . . . joy . . . peace . . . patience . . . kindness . . . goodness . . . trustfulness . . . gentleness . . . self-control.

'Come, O Holy Spirit and kindle in me the fire of your love.'

THE ASSUMPTION

Christ has in fact been raised from the dead, the first-fruits of all who have fallen asleep. Death came through one man and in the same way the resurrection of the dead has come through one man. Just as all men die in Adam, so all men will be brought to life in Christ; but all of them in their proper order: Christ as the first-fruits and then, after the coming of Christ, those who belong to him.

God loved us with so much love that he was generous with his mercy: when we were dead through our sins, he brought us to life with Christ – it is through grace that you have been saved – and raised us up with him and gave us a place with him in heaven, in Christ Jesus. This was to show for all ages to come, through his goodness towards us in Christ Jesus, how infinitely rich he is in grace. Because it is by grace that you have been saved, through faith; not by anything of your own, but by a gift from God; not by anything that you have done, so that nobody can claim the credit. We are God's work of art, created in Christ Jesus to live the good life as from the beginning he had meant us to live it.

1 Corinthians 15: 20–23; Ephesians 2: 4–10

In a very special way Mary is God's work of art.
Alone of creation she lived the good life
as from the beginning she was called by God to live it.

Like all works of art she was irreplaceable . . . inde-structible . . . incorruptible. She was unscathed and untouched by the sin of the world that she lived in . . . she knew not sin . . . and so conquered the one who fathers death.

Mary immaculate, star of the morning,
chosen before the creation began,
chosen to bring, for your bridal adorning,
woe to the serpent and rescue to man.

She was chosen to be
the mother of the Lord . . . who would triumph over
sin and death;
the second Eve . . . bringing not death but life to
men;
the new mother of Mankind . . . taking all into her
heart.

After her Son – 'the first-fruits of all who have fallen
asleep' – she was brought to life in Christ. It was by
God's grace that she was saved, for all are given life by
God's free gift.

She was full of grace . . . supremely free to choose . . .
wholly willing to walk the passage of earthly life to the
incomparable life of glory.

In my daily life I have
to struggle against temptation . . .
to endure the suffering that comes to everyone . . .
to bring woe to the serpent and rescue to my
neighbour . . .
to be able to say 'Amen' to God's will for me . . .
to learn the secrets of the good life to which I am
called.

But by God's grace I am what I am . . . his grace is
sufficient for me . . . he never allows me to be tempted
beyond my strength . . . he offers me unbounded grace,
real freedom, strength and companionship.

Like Mary I am invited to bring forth Christ to the
world . . . to share God's life . . . to be with him . . . to
live as from the beginning he meant me to live.

And all is gift.

'Grace has brought me safe thus far,
and grace will lead me home.'

OUR LADY, QUEEN OF HEAVEN

Near the cross of Jesus stood his mother. Seeing his mother and the disciple he loved standing near by, Jesus said to his mother, 'Woman, this is your son'. Then to the disciple he said, 'This is your mother'. And from that moment the disciple made a place for her in his home.

After that I saw a huge number, impossible to count, of people from every nation, race, tribe and language; they were standing in front of the throne and in front of the Lamb, dressed in white robes and holding palms in their hands. They shouted aloud, 'Victory to our God, who sits on the throne, and to the Lamb!' And all the angels who were standing in a circle round the throne prostrated themselves before the throne, and touched the ground with their foreheads, worshipping God with these words, 'Amen. Praise and glory and wisdom and thanksgiving and honour and power and strength to our God for ever and ever.   Amen.'   John 19: 25–27; Revelation 7: 9–12

The picture I may have of heaven need not bother me. know I cannot even begin to imagine it and that n language can describe it for me. It is enough to appreci ate the promise of the past and the reality of presen hope.

The past is made by those who have gone before,
    the great men and women who lived before Christ, ir hope for his coming . . .
    the mother of Christ, who was blessed because she believed in God's promise . . .
    the apostles and disciples of Jesus, who came to believe that he was the Promised One . . .
    the Christian saints, who have heard the Word of God and kept it . . .
    the men and women of good will, who have searched for what is right and good and have found God.

To these, 'a number impossible to count', the risen Lord has already said: 'Come you blessed of my Father, into the kingdom prepared for you from the foundation of the world.' The word of God was sown in them and they brought forth good fruit.

Mary is their queen,
> the mother who belongs to all, because she gave her Son to the world . . .
> the daughter who gives courage to all, because of God's faithfulness to her . . .
> the virgin who gives hope to all, because of the fruitfulness of her poverty . . .
> the woman who brings comfort to all, because she believed and was saved . . .

What is my present hope?
> that God is with me, cares for me, guides me, loves me, and asks me to make my home with him . . .
> that he has given me, for the time being, charge of the world he made, to help me grow in wisdom and grace . . .
> that he has placed me in a world peopled by other men and women, my brothers and sisters, so that together we may love and serve him . . .
> that his friends who have lived in this world before me, among them especially Mary the mother of God, are my friends . . .
> that together we belong to God and to one another, and are in communion of mind, heart and soul . . .

With such a hope, I am indeed greatly blessed.

> 'Pray for me, a sinner,
> now and at the hour of my death. Amen.'

_____

A Meditation on the Beatitudes

'Be perfect
as your heavenly Father is perfect.'

Lord I hear you say,
'Be perfect as your heavenly Father is perfect',
and I am afraid.
I cannot do what you ask;
you don't expect me to be like God himself?
You know, Lord, that I can never be perfect.
Why do you ask me then even to try?

Perhaps you can't be perfect yet,
but you can always grow.
So set your sights high,
don't refuse to walk a bit further,
or say you have no more to give.

Never be anxious about your weaknesses;
always know that I will give you strength;
try to forgive even those who don't forgive you;
learn what it is to be free;
try not to think evil of others;
be compassionate towards your fellow-men;
be generous and unstinted in your love;
live from moment to moment
without worrying about tomorrow.

You can always walk this step,
and this step is the only one that matters.
To be perfect is not to have achieved all,
but to put no limits to your giving,
to draw no horizon to what is possible,
never to say 'Thus far and no further'.

If you can become like that
you will learn what it is to be like God.

So here is a pattern for your living
– your generous living –
that will bring you true and lasting happiness:

> Blessed are the poor in spirit,
> for theirs is the kingdom of heaven.
>
> Blessed are those who mourn,
> for they shall be comforted.
>
> Blessed are the meek,
> for they shall inherit the earth.
>
> Blessed are those who hunger and thirst for righteous-
> ness,
> for they shall be satisfied.
>
> Blessed are the merciful,
> for they shall obtain mercy.
>
> Blessed are the pure in heart,
> for they shall see God.
>
> Blessed are the peacemakers,
> for they shall be called sons of God.
>
> Blessed are those who are persecuted for righteousness'
> sake,
> for theirs is the kingdom of heaven.

Matthew 5: 2–10

Help me, Lord, to accept this demanding law,
that completes the law of Sinai.
Help me not to be angry with my brother,
not to lust with my mind and heart after another,
to speak the truth,
to be honest and sincere,
to offer good in return for evil,
to give to those who ask,
to trust in your goodness and care,
and to praise and thank you always.   Amen.

**'Blessed are the poor in spirit,
for theirs is the kingdom of heaven.'**

There are times, Lord, when I know how poor I really
   am.
I know that without you I have nothing and I am
   nothing,
and I am happy in this knowledge.
But these times are rare.
More often, in my pride, I try to live alone –
I forget you and ignore my friends.

> Even if you forget me,
> I shall never forget you,
> because I love you
> as tenderly as a mother loves her child.
> To be poor is just to let me be with you,
> to empty yourself of the junk,
> so that I have room in your life.
> I promise that you will never then be in need
> of the things that matter.
> Learn to be content with who you are,
> to be able to live with your failings,
> to be glad about your strengths,
> to rejoice in the goodness of others.
> This is humility,
> this is poverty.
> Be like the child
> who is generous in giving and receiving,
> who is glad to be everyone's friend.
> Poverty is a good platform for friendship.

Lord, what of the good things of life,
of food and drink, of money, security and property?
How can I have these
and still deserve the reward of the poor?

These are gifts,
and every good gift comes from me.
It is how you use them that is important –
do you use them for yourself or for others?
Accept the things of creation
and the work of human hands
gladly and responsibly.
Be honest,
share with those in need,
give generously and without anxiety.
Give of yourself,
your time, your skill, your enthusiasm,
your kindness, your forgiveness, your compassion.
Let go, empty yourself, surrender yourself to me,
then surely you will discover one day
the pearl of great price,
and will be at peace.

———————

Lord, if at times I try to serve two masters,
be patient with me.
Teach me to recognise what is of real value
and not to worry about success, praise or material
    reward.
Plant in me the seed of poverty
so that one day I may hear your call
to leave all things and follow you.   Amen.

**'Blessed are those who mourn,
for they shall be comforted.'**

I'm not sure, Lord,
whether my sadness is true mourning,
or just self-pity and depression.
I'm ashamed of my failures,
scared of being hurt,
afraid that I'll be punished for my sins,
overwhelmed when I realise what you are asking of
    me.

I was afraid too, you know.
It's human to be scared or overwhelmed,
but try not to be afraid of being human,
and remember always that you are loved
with a tremendous love.
The things that worry you
– your shame, self-anger and fear –
are only dangerous if that is where you stop.
I'm asking you to look beyond yourself
towards God, your Father, who loves you
and asks for your love and trust;
and towards the whole company of your fellow men
    and women
with their problems and anxieties –
they too ask for your love and trust.
Love God and love your neighbour as yourself.

Mourn for your sinfulness and failure
because you have been less than you are capable of
    being,
less than what God has called you to be,
and so have weakened the bond of brotherhood.
Your generous, unselfish sorrow,
that accepts responsibility
and seeks forgiveness from your Father
and from your brethren,
will indeed be comforted.

No one can refuse unselfish sorrow.

Mourn, too, with those who suffer:
with the sick, the lonely and depressed,
with the anxious and those who have no friends,
with the apparent failures of the world.
Be aware of them, care for them as best you can,
suffer with them, pray with them, weep with them.
Such real compassion brings its own reward,
of acceptance, trust and healing.
Give, and there will be gifts for you:
a full measure,
pressed down, shaken together, and running over,
will be poured into your lap;
because the amount you measure out
is the amount you will be given back.

Lord, help me to see myself
as a true member of your family,
and to know that others depend on me
as I do on them.
Bring me to a self-forgetful sorrow,
and to an unsparing compassion,
so that in learning to mourn
I may discover the comfort of your presence.   Amen.

**'Blessed are the meek
for they shall inherit the earth.'**

Meek, Lord? What does it mean?

If you think of those who aren't meek
you'll see its meaning clearly enough.
The sharp person who trades in unkind words;
the perfectionist who finds fault in everything;
the boaster who never listens to others;
the jealous man who is afraid of your cleverness;
the authoritarian who plays everything by the rule
    book;
the older person who damps the fire of your
    enthusiasm;
the younger person who is impatient of your
    slowness.
These sad people inherit bitterness, loneliness
    and fear;
they stand on their own platform and isolate
    themselves from others.

To be meek is to have discovered a quiet strength.
Learn of me for I am meek and humble of heart.

Tame yourself,
find the balance of your life,
look for the strength of self-control.
Know that anger can be a gift –
not the violence of unbridled and selfish passion,
but the force that impels you to right what is wrong.

If you are corrected for wrong-doing
accept the reproach without seeking to justify
    yourself;
do not look for revenge;
be courteous towards your accusers.

Use the power you have
to set people free, and not to enslave;

blow gently on the smouldering flax;
be ready with praise and speak generously of others.

Listen sympathetically to excuses;
accept an apology unhesitatingly;
try to understand the other person's feelings;
be gentle towards those who are fearful;
act always with feeling care.

Appreciate the idealism of the young;
heed the wisdom of the old;
be patient with young and old alike;
listen attentively to authority.

Tamed by God,
you will inherit a world of peace,
where nothing can harm you,
and every man is your friend.

———————

Lord, forgive me for my unkindness –
for the harsh and thoughtless things I do and say.
Give me the grace of self-control
and the strength to be gentle,
so that, learning to be meek and humble of heart,
I may be a friend to the friendless
and a support for the weak.   Amen.

**'Blessed are those who hunger and thirst for
   righteousness,
for they shall be satisfied.'**

Lord, I do care about justice,
and try to act justly towards others.
I'm honest about money, and usually tell the truth;
I give a certain amount to charity.
I want people to be free and to be fully alive.
I get angry when I read of torture and cruelty,
and I deplore the dishonesty and callousness I see in
   the world.
Then I remember the parable about the pharisee and
   the publican,
and I wonder . . .

It is good to care about justice
and to work in whatever way you can
to bring greater freedom to the world.
But the justice I want you to practise and proclaim
is something deeper than you may yet have
   discovered.
The just man is the one who is at rights with God and
   men.
He knows that God loves him
and is always beckoning him to come closer;
he lives with God as with a familiar friend,
confident that love covers a multitude of sins;
he knows that God loved the world so much
that he sent his only Son,
so that all who believe in him would be saved.
He has learned, too, to love his enemy;
he offers the wicked man no resistance;
he is quick to forgive those who have hurt him;
he gives to those who ask, and lends without
   question.
He has set his heart on the things of God,
content that God's gifts will bring him deep
   happiness.

The grace you need to pray for
is not just to care about justice,
but to be able to hunger and thirst for what is right,
to be urgent, anxious and aching to be made right by
    God,
to be willing to spend yourself utterly in the quest for
    righteousness.
It is the grace to speak freely with outcasts without
    shame,
to be prepared to see the good of others, whoever they
    may be,
to have the courage to be thought a fool for my sake,
to have a heart big enough to contain the world.

Your search for justice is your search for God.
Ask, and it will be given to you;
search, and you will find;
knock, and the door will be opened to you.

Be sure that you will have your fill:
in justifying others you yourself will be justified;
by easing another's burden you will be made free;
in leading your friend to God your search will be
    satisfied.

———————

Lord, you know how half-hearted I am in my search,
and how often I blind myself to what is truly right.
Forgive my lack of urgency and eagerness.
Set me on fire with your Spirit,
show me the path of justice,
and give me the vision and courage to live as your
    disciple.   Amen.

**'Blessed are the merciful,
for they shall obtain mercy.'**

Have I ever the chance, Lord, to be merciful?
Isn't this something for people with authority,
like judges, magistrates, the police, teachers, or
    employers?
I don't have power over others,
so how can I show mercy?

You often ask for mercy:
you pray, 'Lord, have mercy';
but do you realise what you are asking for?
It should be more than a plea not to be punished,
or for the scales of justice to be balanced in your
    favour.
God is not a magistrate or an employer
who has to apply the law rigorously
and treat everyone according to what they deserve.
He is your Father.
He is full of compassion and love,
and he has made a promise with you
that come what may he will never disown you.
He will not forget you or leave you;
he will always be faithful and steadfast.
This is his mercy –
his promise to reach out to poor, weak, and sinful
    men,
so that with his free gift they may live.
Your prayer for mercy is a reminder to God
for him to fulfill his promise to you –
to be compassionate, patient, forgiving, loving
    towards you.

Mercy is a truly godly quality.
It enriches the bond between you and your friends –
    and enemies.
If you would be great, practise mercy towards others.

Remember the parable about the unforgiving debtor,
who, though his own huge debt was cancelled,
demanded payment from his fellow-worker –
and learn to forgive as often as you are injured.

Read the story of the latecomers to the vineyard,
who, because of the generosity of their employer,
were paid the same wages as the rest –
and discover the love that exceeds justice.

Recall the wounded man who, ignored by his friends,
was cared for by his enemy, the Samaritan –
and know that it is in deeds that mercy is shown.

In all your dealings with others,
whether as one in authority or not,
be aware of them as your companions in the Lord;
understand their strengths and weaknesses, their
    burdens and gifts;
be tolerant of their failures
as you would want them to be tolerant of yours.
Your trust in them will help them trust in you;
your faithfulness to them will encourage them to
    love.

Your mercy will be twice blessed:
'It blesseth him that gives, and him that takes.'

––––––––––––

Lord, be merciful to me a sinner!
Through the experience of your mercy to me
may my love for others become more generous.
May it be a practical love that responds to what is
    needed,
a forgiving love that does not impose conditions,
and an understanding love that sustains the weary
    soul.   Amen.

**'Blessed are the pure in heart,
for they shall see God.'**

Lord, you search me and you know me,
you know my deepest thoughts and feelings.
So often I do those things I don't want to do,
and fail to do what in my inmost heart I eagerly desire.
I pray for purity of mind and heart and body,
yet my prayer seems unanswered.
Shall I ever see God face to face?

Your cross, which you cannot escape, is yourself.
Accept this burden gratefully and willingly,
and realise that it is a blessing for you
to be this woman or this man.
Like any cross you may want to shrug it off at times;
then come to me and you will find rest for your soul.
If you would be my disciple you must bear with
    yourself.
I shall not let you be tried beyond your strength.

The attraction you have for others and they for you
is something to praise God for,
not to be ashamed or frightened of.
See in it a source of your growth,
and not a threat to your immortality.

Take courage.
What is in your heart is what is most important.
It is from the heart that evil comes,
and if your heart is pure
and the spirit is willing,
then even if the flesh is weak
you shall find forgiveness and hope.

Learn, if you can, from the purity of the child.
There is in him a simplicity and directness
that dissolves all prejudice and anger.
His innocence is a light
that the darkness cannot overpower.

His friendship is for everyone.
His thoughts go with uncomplicated ease
to the heart of the problem.
He is pure, untouched by evil, unadulterated.

Do not judge yourself too harshly.
Strive to be simple and sincere.
Remember the importance of a humble and contrite
    heart.
Do not be anxious about your motives,
but do straightforwardly what you see to be right.

One day your cross will be mounted like mine on
    Calvary,
so that through that final death
you may take up your new life with God.
Then you will know him face to face
and the purity of your heart will at last triumph
over the weakness of your body.
I am the resurrection and the life;
he who believes in me will have eternal life.

———————

Lord, when my eyes are blinded
and my ears are deafened by false attractions,
keep my heart fixed on you.
Help me to find again the sincerity and simplicity
that leads direct to you,
the object of my real desire.   Amen.

**'Blessed are the peacemakers,
for they shall be called sons of God.'**

Lord, you can't open a newspaper or listen to the news
without learning of some new attack on peace.
There's everything from the threat of nuclear war
to statistics on divorce.
How does a follower of yours
even begin to struggle against these evils?

Do you believe that true peace is possible,
or do you in your heart of hearts
think that this is an impossible dream?

There is only one road to peace,
and that is for you to be at peace in yourself
and with your fellow men and women.
Love your neighbour as yourself.
Love your enemy,
do good to those who insult you,
pray for those who persecute and caluminate you.

I came to bring peace.
My work was to build bridges between people,
and to span the gulf between man and God.
It meant trying to break the barriers of prejudice,
healing those who were sick in body, mind and soul,
helping people to realise that they could be free.
If you want to be my disciple
this is your work too.

Your personal peace will come with the knowledge
that you are truly forgiven and redeemed.
My peace I leave you, my peace I give you;
a peace that is more than the ending of conflict,
rather the meeting of minds and hearts
that marks the beginning of reconciliation and
    contentment.
Your certainty that you are safe in God's hands

is what gives you the authority and power to make
   peace.

It will give you the courage to be uncompromising
in confronting violence and slavery.
It will show you the gentleness needed
in healing those hurt by evil.
It will bring you the wisdom and skill
to temper anger and remove suspicion.

You may not sway the world,
remove the threat of war,
decrease the crime rate,
or make marriage more stable.
But be sure that by your actions for peace
the world is thereby blessed.
Without your tears the ocean is the poorer.

If you make peace even in small things,
you are my brother or sister,
and will share my inheritance with the Father.

———————

Lord, give me the strength, confidence and patience
to work for a true and lasting peace.
May I find peace in my own heart,
and bring your peace to family, friends and fellow-
   workers.
Help me to do the small things well
so that the greater may follow,
for your sake and for the world.   Amen.

**'Blessed are those who are persecuted for
righteousness' sake,
for theirs is the kingdom of heaven.'**

I admire the martyrs, Lord, and deeply respect them,
but I'm not that sort of person.
I don't think I'd stand up to persecution,
and in any case I don't really do anything
that people would want to attack me for.

Has anyone ever derided your faith,
attacked your stand for Christian morality,
or smiled at your praying?
Do you ever deny yourself something on my account,
suffer because men pass me by,
or accept the pain of cross-bearing?
If you are faithful in these things
you are already a witness to my name,
and in your witnessing you are a martyr.

If you live up to your Christian calling
you are certain, sooner or later, to be persecuted.
As my disciple you will slowly learn to be different,
to be a sign of contradiction to those
who worship other gods.
Your standards will rebuke the world,
so that your own people will disown you.
Even by your silence you will confront others
and risk their anger and contempt.
You will be in the world, but not of it.

As a member of my own Body
I invite you to speak on my behalf –
boldly, in season and out of season, to prophesy.
I ask you to take your part, by word and action,
in preaching the truth my Father has revealed,
to a world that is hungry for truth.

Embrace this truth yourself;
live according to the truth;

proclaim the truth with conviction;
share the truth willingly.
You can be confident, for I am with you.
I shall send you the Spirit of truth
who will teach you all things
and fill you with the fire of his love.
And the truth will set you free.

When they persecute you,
teach them to love,
for perfect love casts out fear;
and forgive them,
for they know not what they do.

Rejoice and be glad,
for the suffering of the saints brings life to a fallen
    world.
Your reward will be great in heaven.

Lord, I pray for the grace to become a Christian.
Teach me how to live a gospel life:
help me always to stand up for the truth,
and never to condone a lie by my inaction.
May I learn to suffer gladly for bearing your name,
so that the world may know that you have sent me,
and that your word is true.   Amen.

A Meditation on the Way of the Cross

THE FIRST STATION

Jesus is condemned to death

The play-acting that has been taking place is a
perfect example of the weak-minded judge.

Pilate is frightened –
of the Jews, of Caesar, of Christ.

The hand-washing is the crowning sign
of his weakness.

He had power, but would have had no power at all
were it not given from above.

'Judge not and you shall not be judged.'

Yet I often judge others . . .
sometimes needlessly and rashly.

Is it ever for me to judge another man . . .
or his motives?

Can I ever do so rightly?

Perhaps sometimes I have to make a judgement.

Then, Lord, let me do so with real justice,
and with mercy.

Let my motive always be love . . .
love of God and neighbour and not of self.

Help me always to judge others
as I would have them judge me.

Teach me to judge others
as I would have you judge me.

Lord in you mercy

Hear our prayer

THE SECOND STATION

Jesus takes up his cross

A cross is synonymous in our language with a
burden . . . something heavy, unwieldly, unwanted.

Jesus carrying his cross has made the cross
a symbol of victory.

It has become the sign in which we conquer.

We need not think of it as a burden –
'my yoke is sweet, my burden light'.

What is my cross?

It is myself with all my failings, imperfections,
eccentricities.

It is my fears . . .
the fear of facing up to my responsibilities . . .
the fear of boredom with my daily routine . . .
the fear of being found out . . .
the fear of what other people think of me . . .
the fear of loneliness . . .
the fear of failure.

'Take up your cross daily, and come follow me.'

Jesus, I am lumbered with myself . . . help me to
find my feet.

Jesus falls the first time

It is incredible that Jesus Christ, God made man,
should fall down.

We have to remind ourselves that he was man,
'Like us in all things except sin.'

He was born . . . was nursed like any other baby . . .
he grew up, and advanced 'in wisdom and knowledge
and grace before God and man.'

He was subject to the same laws of nature
as ourselves.

He was a man . . . as physically weak as all men
are . . . he knew his weakness: 'My Father, if it
be possible, let this cup pass from me . . .'

Do I know my weakness?

Is it part of my trouble that I think I'm stronger
than I really am?

Am I too impatient in my passage towards God?

Do I stumble through over-confidence?

Help me to know my weakness, Lord, so that I can
overcome the petty faults which keep me from you . . .
my thoughtlessness towards others . . .
my carelessness in prayer . . .
my obstinacy in holding to my own opinion . . .
my impatience and irritability.

Help me, Jesus, to learn by my mistakes, and always
to lean on you.

THE FOURTH STATION

Jesus meets his blessed mother

Can we really imagine this?

The summit of a mother's selflessness –
the giving of her son.

Even if she knew all that was involved it was still a
loss . . .
an inexpressible anguish . . .
a suffering with him in perfect sympathy . . .
a weight of sadness that there was so little she could do
to help . . .
a contentment that she could be with him and comfort
him.

Isn't this often a mother's and a father's sorrow?
The loss, for a time, of their children?

Isn't it, too, a child's sorrow?
To be cut off from his parents by misunder-
standing . . . a desire for freedom from control . . .
loneliness . . . a feeling of being unwanted?

Young people have their own cross to carry
to the top of their own Calvary.

On the way they need the affection, sympathy, security
of their family –
who perhaps, like Mary, can do so little to help.

Help me, Mary, to take my cue from you . . .
to bear, if need be, the sight of my children leaving
me . . . to be with them when I'm needed . . .
to hide from them my own sadness.

Help me, Jesus, to be understanding with my
parents, and to let them help me.

THE FIFTH STATION

Simon of Cyrene helps Jesus to carry his cross

What sort of a man was Simon . . . what did he do
for a living . . . why was he in Jerusalem . . . why
was he watching this sordid procession?

He was probably a very ordinary person like you
or me . . . just in from the country for a day or
two . . . eager to see the city sights . . . inquisitive
for cheap entertainment.

Then he was hauled out from the crowd and forced
to take part in it all.

How did he react?

Surely he was first of all angry and afraid.

This is so often my reaction when I'm pilloried
in any way – anger and fear.

Angry that someone has doubted my word . . .
afraid that perhaps I'm not right after all.

Angry because my little pedestal has been
     upset . . .
afraid that I won't be able to get back on it again.

Angry with the foolishness of others who don't or won't
     hold the same view as me . . .
afraid that I may be made to look more foolish than
     them.

Help me, Lord Jesus, to master my fear and anger,
which so often stems from pride and self-love.

Help me to be at peace with myself, following in
your footsteps.

THE SIXTH STATION

Veronica wipes the face of Jesus

This is a simple act of charity . . .
but splendidly heroic and uniquely rewarded.

I don't have the chance to perform acts like that . . .
indeed, I'm foolish if I think I can.

This is part of my trouble –
I day-dream all the time . . .

I wonder what I would have done . . .
would I have behaved like Veronica . . .
or Simon . . .
or Peter . . .
or Judas . . .

But such wondering is fruitless.

All I need to ask is whether I do, here and now,
behave like Veronica.

If I do, the reward is the same . . .
I receive the imprint of Christ on my life.

'Put on then, as God's chosen ones, holy and be-
loved, compassion . . . kindness . . . lowliness . . .
meekness . . . patience . . . forbearing one another
. . . forgiving each other.'

'Above all these put on love, which binds everything
together in perfect harmony.'

This is both the reward of our charity
and its cause.

74

THE SEVENTH STATION

Jesus falls the second time

In the garden Jesus prayed:

'My Father, if it be possible, let this cup pass from me;
nevertheless, not as I will, but as thou wilt.'

On the cross he said:

'My God, my God, why hast thou forsaken me?'

Did Jesus have difficulty on the way of the cross?
We take for granted, almost, his perseverance . . .
his trust in his heavenly Father.
But this was genuine perseverance, genuine trust.

There is nothing sham in the humanity of Christ.

My way of the cross is pretty easy by comparison.
Yet I, too, need trust and the grace of perseverance . . .
and especially in the sacrament of penance.

My sins are so routine . . .
I have to confess the same ones again and again . . .
maybe I can take comfort in this . . .
perhaps I'm getting no worse.

I must learn to persevere in my sorrow . . .
to show, by my actions, that my sorrow is real . . .
never to let my conscience become calloused . . .
never to become oblivious to a fault, however slight it
seems to be . . .
never to stop trying.

I must learn to trust more completely in God . . .
to have an unwearied hope that in the end, like Christ,
I shall overcome.
After all, God has promised me just that.

THE EIGHTH STATION

The women of Jerusalem mourn for Jesus

These were kind people who were genuinely sad to
see such suffering. But in spite of their sincerity
and kindness they missed the point. 'Was it not
necessary that the Christ should suffer these things
and enter into his glory?'

Do I mourn about the right things?

'Woe upon you who laugh now,
you shall mourn and weep.'
'Blessed are you who weep now,
you will laugh for joy.'

There is so much false joy in the world –
escapism . . . ridicule . . . irony . . . facetiousness . . .
the degrading of human virtue . . . mockery . . .
pleasure seeking.

This is only a preparation for tears.

Sorrow can lead to misery . . . to bitterness . . .
to despair . . . to frustration . . .
to rejection of the truth.

This sorrow is without faith . . . or hope . . .
or charity.

In our sorrow we can always come to God . . . 'You
who weep now come to this God, for he is weeping.'
By our tears we make up what is lacking in the sorrows of Christ. This can be the true sorrow that
leads us to joy. The joy that we are part of God's
plan, that we can share in the Incarnation . . . in the
Redemption.

Joy is the keynote of Christian spirituality. The
gospel is the good news of great joy. The origin of
our joy is the Incarnation . . . 'the God who became
man, that man might become God.'

Jesus falls the third time

We can scarcely blame the onlookers if they failed
to see this as a triumphal journey. The psalmist's
description is accurate enough –

> 'I am a worm and not a man,
>   the scorn of men and despised of the people.
> I am poured out like water,
>   and all my bones are disjointed.
> My heart has become like wax,
>   melting away within my breast.
> My throat is dried up like a potsherd,
>   my tongue cleaves to my jaws,
>   and in the dust of death you have laid me.'

A description, in its way, of me.
Weak of will . . .
lax of conscience . . .
dry of love.
In such a state I deserve to be despised.

I need both goading and encouraging.

You speak to me, Lord, when I pray –
encourage me to listen to you patiently.

You speak to me, Lord, when I am reading or listening
    to a sermon –
encourage me to listen humbly . . . intelligently . . .
without undue criticism. Unless I become as a
little child, I shall not enter into the kingdom of
heaven.

Lord, goad me to perfection.

THE TENTH STATION

Jesus is stripped of his clothes

By way of humiliation this was the last straw.

'Who, though he was in the form of God,
did not count equality with God a thing to be grasped,
but emptied himself,
taking the form of a servant,
being born in the likeness of men.

And being found in human form,
he humbled himself,
and became obedient unto death,
even death on a cross.'

He did not prize his possessions,
neither those due to him as God . . .
nor those due to him as man.

He had no home . . .
was often hungry and thirsty . . .
was born in poverty . . . and died in poverty.

I like to pretend to myself that I am poor in spirit.
But sometimes I find myself terribly concerned
about trivialities –
Can I afford a new fridge? . . . a new car? . . . a new
    suit? . . .
Should I take out another insurance policy? . . .
Will I get a rise next week . . . month . . . year?

I know well enough that I'm not a lily of the field
and that I must toil and spin, but I wonder whether
I'm often over-concerned about taking care for
tomorrow?

Help me, Lord Jesus, to be genuinely poor in
spirit . . . to find a proper balance between caution
and recklessness . . . to deepen my understanding
of Providence.

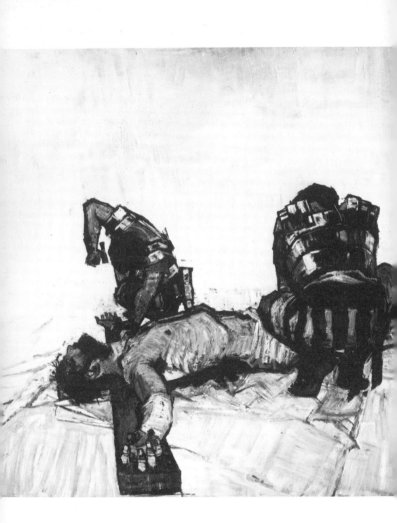

THE ELEVENTH STATION

Jesus is nailed to the cross

It is the sheer, unmitigated cruelty of it which
disgusts us first of all. It seems unbelievable that man,
created in the image and likeness of God, should be
able to sink to such depths.
We call such acts barbaric, inhuman.

Cruelty survives today on the grand scale –
the concentration camps . . .
the violence of modern crime . . .
the savage cruelty of some towards their children.

With me it may be a question of motes and beams
turned back to front. I am so scandalised by the
viciousness of some, that I scarcely notice the speck
of inhumanity in myself –
my barbed wit . . .
my lack of charity towards motorists or pedestrians . . .
my ignoring of those I don't want to like . . .
my willingness to gossip and say something hurtful . . .
my condescension towards those more ignorant than
    myself . . .
my impatience with those younger – or older – than
    myself . . .

Pinpricks – which beside Christ's wounds are as
    nothing.
But these are my faults,
for which I am answerable.

Help me, Jesus, to heal the wounds caused by hate,
and to show to all men the love you have shown to
me.

'Forgive us our trespasses as we forgive those who
trespass against us.'

THE TWELFTH STATION

Jesus dies on the cross

'It was about the sixth hour, and there was
darkness over the whole land until the ninth hour,
while the sun's light failed; and the curtain of the
temple was torn in two. Then Jesus, crying out
with a loud voice, said, "Father, into thy hands
I commend my spirit!" And having said this he
breathed his last.'

'Without beauty, without majesty (we saw him),
no looks to attract our eyes;
a thing despised and rejected by men,
a man of sorrows and familiar with suffering.
And yet ours were the sufferings he bore,
ours the sorrows he carried.'

'Greater love has no man than this,
that a man lay down his life for his friends.'

'I am the Lord your God . . . your Saviour . . .
you are precious in my eyes . . . and I love you . . .

Fear not, for I am with you . . .
you are my witnesses . . .
my chosen people . . .
the people whom I formed for myself . . .

Turn to me and be saved, for I am God . . .
Return to me, for I have redeemed you.'

'And I, when I am lifted up from the earth,
will draw all men to myself.'

'Unless a grain of wheat falls into the earth and dies,
it remains alone; but if it dies, it bears much fruit.'

THE THIRTEENTH STATION

Jesus is taken down from the cross

'Like us in all things except sin'.

The dead body of Jesus. It is hard to take this in . . .
that Jesus really died . . . that his body became a
lifeless thing . . . an empty shell.

If we have seen death we know how unreal a dead
body looks. It is so obviously empty . . . incomplete
. . . utterly different from what it was a few moments
before.

And yet, 'Truly this was the Son of God.'

I wouldn't be human if I were entirely unafraid of
   death.

The saint may say, 'I desire to be dissolved and to be
   with Christ';
but if I say this, the words are a little hollow.

Yet in spite of my natural human fear,
I have hope . . .
Christ has been there before me.

My only wish is that when God calls me
I shall be able to say, like Christ,
'It is finished, the work you gave me is done.'

Help me, Lord Jesus, to approach death unafraid,
confident that I have tried to do your will.

THE FOURTEENTH STATION

Jesus is placed in the tomb

'He descended into hell. The third day he rose again
from the dead. He ascended into heaven and sits
on the right hand of God the almighty Father . . .'
continually interceding on our behalf.

The grave is only a passing resting place . . .
for us as for Christ.

The life, death, resurrection and ascension of
Jesus Christ is the promise for us of eternal life.

We are one body with Christ –
we are no longer alone in our pursuit for God . . .
we go with Christ . . .
we go as other Christs . . .

We share each other's blessings and burdens –
forgetful of self . . .
filled with the same hope . . .
fired with the same faith . . .
united in the same love for each other and for God.

I pray that in my life I may mirror Christ –
that I may truly die to sin . . .
that I may make my daily round my daily prayer . . .
that by my love I may lead others to Christ . . .
that in my God-given vocation I may be all things to all
men.

I know that my Redeemer lives, and that through
him, with him and in him, all of us shall find life.

An Examination of Conscience

Every now and then it is valuable for us to pause and look at ourselves, so as to see how we are living. It may be helpful to do this by reflecting on our Lord's teaching – for instance, the Beatitudes, one of the parables, or the account of the Last Judgement. Tradition suggests that the Portrait of Love given by St Paul (1 Corinthians 13: 4–13) is a description of Jesus himself. So it is given here as a background against which we may see ourselves. If it is used as part of a night prayer, it may well be enough to choose one phrase only to think about.

'Love is always patient and kind' . . .

Am I patient with myself?
Do I expect too much of myself?
Do I get angry with myself when I fail?

Am I impatient in prayer?
Do I stop praying if I don't get quick results?
Do I remember to pray for others?

Am I patient with others?
Do I get irritable at other people's failures or weaknesses or eccentricities, or if they are less quick or clever than me?

Am I patient and kind with children, the elderly and
   sick?
Am I patient with those who work with me or for me?
Do I listen patiently to those in authority?

Am I gentle and kind in my speech?
Do I speak well of others?
Do I act kindly towards those in a less privileged
   position than me?

... 'it is never jealous, boastful or conceited' ...

Am I jealous of someone else's good fortune, or success?
Do I try to keep up with my next door neighbour?
Do I drive my children (or others) so that I can boast of
   them?

   Am I affronted if others don't live up to my
      expectations?
   Do I expect more of others than I do of myself?
   Do I criticise others so that they lose confidence in
      themselves?

Am I complacent about myself?
Am I hypocritical in the way I live?
Do I keep on comparing myself with others?

> Do I look for praise from others?
> Am I slow to thank, to encourage or to praise?
> Do I bore others by talking about myself?

Do I bother to listen to others?
Am I slow to apologise or to admit my faults?
Do I show my gratitude to God and my fellow men for
  all they do for me?

... 'it is never rude or selfish' ...

Do I treat others with the respect due to them as
  persons?
Am I chaste in my relationships with others?
Do I sin against purity in mind or action?

> Does my language reflect my human dignity?
> Am I ever arrogant, obstinate or overbearing?
> Does my chattering prevent others from speaking?

Do I insist on what I want before thinking about
  others?
Do I inconvenience others by my selfish use of
  transistor, TV or record player?
Do I consider the effect that my actions will have on
  others?

> Do I take a genuine interest in the needs of the Third
>   World?
> Is my attitude to material things determined by
>   selfish motives?
> Do I use my own and other people's property with
>   due care?

Do I ever deliberately hurt another?
Do I seek for pleasure at the expense of others?
Does my selfishness ever lead me to ignore God?

. . . 'it does not take offence, and is not resentful' . . .

Am I touchy about my rights?
Am I prepared to accept criticism?
Do I feel slighted if others are preferred to me?

> How do I react to my failures?
> How do I respond if I am unjustly treated or misunderstood?
> Am I willing to accept injustice as Christ did, with meekness?

What is my attitude to law; do I ignore it if it inconveniences me?
Do I impose laws on others that I am not prepared to keep myself?
Do I act on what Christ said: 'If you love me you will keep my commandments'?

> Do I forgive those who sin against me?
> Do I ask forgiveness from those whom I have sinned against?
> Am I resentful at the way God treats me?

Do I drive others to resentment by harshness, unreasonableness, thoughtlessness, or selfishness?
Am I resentful of my own weaknesses?
Do I resent my dependence on others and on God?

. . . 'Love delights in truth' . . .

Am I a truthful person?
Do I try to grow in the understanding of truth?
Do I pray for God's Spirit of truth in my life?

> Do I repeat what I hear without bothering to verify its truth or falsity?
> Do I gossip, or spread rumours, or scandal?
> Do I hide or distort truth by my speech, my actions or my silence?

An Examination of Conscience

Do I respect those who sincerely hold different beliefs
   to mine?
Do I try to understand the beliefs of others?
Do I allow others freedom to accept truth, or do I put
   unjust pressures on them?

   Do I witness by word and example to the truth of the
      Gospel?
   As a teacher do I take the trouble to learn?
   Do I ever compromise the truth for fear of what
      others may think?

Is my life a true reflection of my beliefs?
Do I try to share my vision of truth with others?
Do I look and listen for God in my life?

**... 'it is always ready to excuse, to trust, to
hope' ...**

Do I take Christ's advice: 'Judge not and you shall not
   be judged'?
Am I quicker to judge others than I am to judge
   myself?
Do I try to understand the actions of others?

   Do I make excuses for myself when I sin?
   Am I able to forgive myself?
   Do I have a firm hope that God will give me his
      grace?

Am I ready to accept others whatever their faults?
Am I willing to trust others even when they let me
   down?
Do I help others to grow and to hope by putting my
   trust in them?

   Do I see justice and mercy as being in conflict?
   Am I rigid in my application of the law?
   Am I ready to be generous in forgiving?

Do I accept that I shall not be tried beyond my
   strength?

Do I believe that nothing can separate me from the love of God?

Am I able to accept my weaknesses, knowing that Christ's strength will work in me?

... 'it is always ready to endure whatever comes' ...

Do I grumble about the problems and hardships of my life?

Do I accept that true love will always bring suffering?

Am I prepared to take up my cross daily and follow Christ?

How do I try to face doubt?

Do I try to overcome my own bad habits?

Do I lose hope when it seems everyone is against me?

Does my love for those close to me overcome their unkindnesses, their weaknesses, their letting me down, their failures?

Is my love for those who hurt me such that I can forgive them?

Do I blame God for my sufferings and difficulties?

Is my love for God such that I can accept persecution for speaking out in his name?

Do I realise that to love another means to die to self?

Do I accept that there are three things that last: faith, hope and love, and that the greatest of these is love?